THE
Bulletproof George Washington

DAVID BARTON

Aledo, Texas

Additional materials available from:
WallBuilders
P.O. Box 397
Aledo, TX 76008
(817) 441-6044
For orders or to obtain a catalog, call (800) 873-2845
www.wallbuilders.com

Cover portrait:
Washington Rallying the Troops at Monmouth by Emmanuel Leutze (detail); Courtesy, University of California, Berkeley Art Museum; Gift of Mrs. Mark Hopkins; Photographer, Benjamin Blackwell

Library of Congress Cataloging-in-Publication Data
Barton, David.
The Bulletproof George Washington / David Barton. – 2nd ed.
64 p; 21 cm
Includes timeline of events, sources of illustrations, endnotes and price list.

1. Washington, George, President U.S. 1732-1799.   2. Monongahela, Battle of the, 1725.   I. Title.
973.2/6   LOC 91-107126

ISBN 0-932225-00-5

Table of Contents

Introduction and Foreword

George Washington, "The Father of his Country," is well known for the accomplishments of his adult life: commander-in-chief during the American Revolution, a statesman guiding the writing of the Constitution, and our first President. Yet it was his younger years that formed the character and shaped the destiny of our national hero as an adult (a wise maxim observes, "As the sapling is bent, so goes the tree"). Regrettably, few Americans know much about Washington's youth beyond perhaps the folklore concerning the cherry tree incident. For this reason, the account of what happened to and around the young George Washington during the 1755 battle on the Monongahela is so very important.

Washington was a 23 year-old colonel at the time, and the events of this dramatic battle helped confirm God's special call on this young man as his life literally hung in the balance for over two hours. In fact, fifteen years after that battle, the chieftain of the Indians whom Washington fought on that day sought him out in order to relate his perspective of what had occurred during the battle:

> I am a chief and ruler over my tribes. My influence extends to the waters of the great lakes and to the far blue mountains. I have traveled a long and weary path that I might see the young warrior of the great battle. It was on the day when the white man's blood mixed with the streams of our forest that I first beheld this chief [Washington]. . . . I called to my young men and said. . . . Quick, let your aim be certain, and he dies. Our rifles were leveled, rifles which, but for you, knew not how to miss — 'twas all in vain, a power mightier far than we shielded you. . . . I am come to pay homage to the man who is the particular favorite of Heaven, and who can never die in battle.

While few today have ever heard this intriguing story (much less the amazing details that caused the chieftain to reach his conclusion), this account was well known in the early days of our republic.

This is confirmed by the dozens of older historical texts which I consulted for this work.

Numerous sources provide details of this momentous event, including Washington's personal writings, the records of other participants in that battle, the details provided by Benjamin Franklin in his autobiography, and the research of prominent historians of earlier generations. The excerpts from these historical accounts (some of which were first published two-and-a-half centuries ago), as well as that from many early school texts, have been woven together in this narrative to provide both an accurate account of the battle and exciting and informative reading. (Several pictorial illustrations from those early works have also been included.)

Through this account you will gain a greater appreciation for the Father of our Country and a profound respect for the manner in which God sovereignly selected him and directly intervened on his behalf, preserving him for the important task of helping bring forth, guide, and stabilize this great nation. The words spoken long ago by God to his beloved servant David seem also to be descriptive of the manner in which God used George Washington:

> I took you . . . to be a ruler over my people. . . . I have been with you wherever you have gone. . . . Now I will make your name like the names of the greatest men of the earth.
> *1 Chronicles 17:7–8, NIV*

May this account once again become widely celebrated throughout America!

David Barton

Chapter 1

The French & Indian War

In the seventy-five years from 1688 to 1763, England and France grappled in several European wars. In 1754, their fourth war erupted, this time involving the American colonies. England and France both had settlements in America, and this war pitted the Americans and the British against the French and her Indian allies. Known as the French and Indian War, this was the final struggle between the two nations for colonial supremacy in America. It also heralded a new epoch in American history, marking the first time that the colonies acted together in concert.

The individual American colonies had long been kept apart by their own prejudices, suspicions, and mutual jealousies. But because of the Great Awakening, and especially due to the work of the Rev. George Whitefield and his famous "Father Abraham" sermon that

THE REV. GEORGE WHITEFIELD

he preached throughout the country, the Americans discovered that the colonies had much in common. Many old antagonisms passed away and a new generation arose with a fresh viewpoint. The colonies began to view each other as friends and allies rather than enemies or competitors; they actually began to cooperate with each other, cultivating more tolerant sentiments. Consequently, when the danger from the French and the Indians arose, the colonists mutually joined together against their common foe. During the French and Indian war the separate histories of the colonies for the first time became lost in the more general history of the emerging nation.

Although armed hostilities began in 1754, the primary cause of the war had existed for years: long-standing territorial conflicts between England and France.

For ambitious nations, acquiring large portions of the American continent was extremely desirable. Here was a country extending thousands of miles, covered by vast forests able to supply abundant timber to meet the demands of a growing world, containing boundless stores of mineral wealth, with a climate varied enough to support diverse types of production. It was not surprising that nations across the ocean were eager to obtain as large a share of these benefits as possible.

The English located their settlements primarily along the Atlantic sea coast from Maine to Florida, but their claims reached far inland. English kings proceeded upon the theory that the voyage of Sebastian Cabot gave them a lawful right to America from the Atlantic all the way westward to the Pacific, so their territorial claims were not limited to what they actually occupied.

Since the French also had been early explorers and settlers of the continent, they too felt that they had a special claim to a generous share of the New World. Unlike England, however, France had colonized the interior of the continent, and early French settlements such as Montreal and Detroit were more than five hundred miles inland from the Atlantic. Their territorial claims clashed directly with those of England.

Had the French limited their claims to the northern settlements along the St. Lawrence River and its tributaries near what is now the Canadian border, there would have been little danger of territorial conflicts. But the French settlements were widely separated along the interior, stretching from Canada all the way south to Louisiana and New Orleans. The Governor of Canada proposed connecting these widely separated colonies by a chain of forts extending along the Ohio and Mississippi Rivers — occupying lands already claimed by the English. The French therefore pushed their way southward from the Great Lakes to the Illinois River, the Mississippi River, and finally the Gulf of Mexico.

Their purpose was to divide the American continent, drawing a barrier against the English settlements on the eastern seaboard. If the French could keep the English east of the Allegheny mountains (from New York in the north to Virginia in the south), they could possess the larger portion of the continent for France. To accomplish this goal became the driving ambition of the French; to prevent it, the stubborn purpose of the English.

The English fur traders of Virginia and Pennsylvania had long frequented Indian villages on the upper tributaries of the Ohio and had established several trading posts stretching inland from the Atlantic coast to the Ohio River. The Indians became accustomed to bringing their furs to these points to exchange them for English trinkets and goods. However, the French traders of Canada began to visit those same villages to compete with the English in the purchase of furs. But because the Virginia colony had already claimed the Ohio territory, the French fur traders were regarded as intruders not to be tolerated.

TRADING WITH THE INDIANS

To prevent further French encroachment, several prominent Virginians formally established The Ohio Company, the purpose of which was to occupy the disputed territory permanently. Robert Dinwiddie (the Governor of Virginia), Laurence and Augustus Washington (George's elder stepbrothers from his father's first marriage), and Thomas Lee (president of the Virginia Council) were its principal members.

The French, however, were equally enterprising. Before the Ohio Company could dispatch a group of settlers to take control of the Ohio Valley area, the Governor of Canada dispatched three hundred men to occupy that valley; signs were nailed on trees; and plates of lead bearing French inscriptions were buried at numerous locations along both banks of the Ohio warning all who saw them that the country belonged to France. The French also began building a line of forts along the Allegheny River in northwestern Pennsylvania. They even wrote a letter to Governor Hamilton of Pennsylvania warning him to encroach no further into the territory of the king of France — territory actually in his Pennsylvania colony.

ONE OF THE LEAD PLATES BURIED BY THE FRENCH ON THE BANKS OF THE OHIO RIVER

To the French, the English trading posts were viewed as obstructions to French plans. Because those trading posts were symbols of English jurisdiction and well known to the Indians, they had to be destroyed — or seized and converted to the use of the French. Accordingly, English trading posts were attacked and pillaged by the French, and English traders were made prisoners. The English, however, would not permit themselves to be outdone in hostile activity. They responded in kind, regularly raiding French Acadian farmers and fishermen off the coast of Newfoundland, Canada, deporting them to the French settlement of New Orleans.

The attempts by both nations to secure possession of the same territory continued to escalate. The French fortified new positions along the Allegheny, Ohio, and Mississippi Rivers between their northern colony of Quebec and their southern settlement of New Orleans; and the English, in the summer of 1753, opened a road through the mountains into the Ohio Valley and planted a new English settlement. It was obvious that open conflict could not be averted much longer.

Chapter 2

George Washington
and the Great Meadows

Before proceeding to war, Virginia's Governor Dinwiddie decided to file a final diplomatic objection with the French. A formal document was drawn up setting forth the nature and extent of the English claim to the Ohio Valley, sternly warning the French against further intrusion into that region.

It was necessary that this official remonstrance be carried to the French commander of its western forces, General St. Pierre, stationed at Fort Erie in northwestern Pennsylvania. This would be perhaps the most serious diplomatic mission yet undertaken in America. Who should bear this important parchment to its destination so far away? A young surveyor named George Washington was selected to make the perilous trek. The governor summoned him from his home on the Potomac and commissioned him as ambassador. Washington carried the mes-

WASHINGTON THE SURVEYOR

sage from the seat of government at Williamsburg in southeastern Virginia far north through the untrodden wilderness to Presque Isle

WASHINGTON LEADING THE TRIP TO OHIO

on the shore of Lake Erie in northern Pennsylvania.

The twenty-one year old Washington departed on October 31st, 1753, to traverse more than five hundred miles through the pathless, wintry wilderness. The tiny party, including an interpreter and guide, plunged into the recesses of the wild, leaving behind every vestige of civilization. They endured snow and storms, crossed mountain passes, and traveled through dense forests and into flooded valleys, where they were forced to navigate swollen, raging rivers on frail, dangerous rafts. Arriving at the Youghiogeny River in west-

WASHINGTON CROSSING RAIN-SWOLLEN RIVERS

ern Pennsylvania, they followed it to the Monongahela and then followed that to its junction with the Allegheny. That junction of the Allegheny and Monongahela Rivers was called "The Fork"; it later became the site of the French Fort Duquesne (pronounced Dew-Cane), and then the location of the English Fort Pitt, from which sprang the present city of Pittsburgh. At the time that Washington and his party passed The Fork it was uninhabited; yet he noticed it and later reported it as an excellent site for a fort or a settlement.

From The Fork, Washington continued down the river twenty miles to deliver friendly greetings from Governor Dinwiddie to Chief Tanacharison (also called the Half-King), the leader of the Southern Hurons, whose friendship was being sought by both the French and the English. The chief received him with kindness, and after Washington had attended a friendly council with the Indians, Tanacharison and three of his men accompanied Washington north the remaining hundred miles to the French encampment. Here, on December 12th,

WASHINGTON IN THE FRENCH FORT

at Fort le Boeuf, Washington found the French general, St. Pierre.

Washington was admitted with great politeness, but the French general refused to enter into any discussion on the rights of England. He was acting, he explained, under military instructions given him by the governor of New

France. He had been commanded to eject every Englishman from the Ohio Valley and he meant to carry out his orders to the letter. France claimed the Ohio territory by virtue of discovery, exploration, and occupation; her claim now would be made good by force of arms. The French commander then composed a written response to be returned to Governor Dinwiddie.

Washington was dismissed, but not before he had noted the immense preparations being made by the French. A fleet of fifty birch-bark canoes and a hundred and seventy pine boats was ready to descend the river to the site of The Fork. It

A FLEET OF CANOES

seemed the French, as well as Washington, had noted the importance of that spot and were determined to fortify it as soon as the ice in the river should break.

THE
JOURNAL
OF
Major *George Washington,*
SENT BY THE
Hon. *ROBERT DINWIDDIE,* Esq;
His Majesty's Lieutenant-Governor, and
Commander in Chief of *VIRGINIA,*
TO THE
COMMANDANT
OF THE
FRENCH FORCES
ON
OHIO.
To which are added, the
GOVERNOR's LETTER,
And A TRANSLATION of the
FRENCH OFFICER's ANSWER

WILLIAMSBURG:
Printed by WILLIAM HUNTER. 1754

WASHINGTON'S JOURNAL

With the mission now completed, Washington's party moved out to hunt and trap while he returned alone to Virginia during the dead of winter. Washington arrived at Williamsburg on January 16th, only eleven weeks after his departure. The boldness, judiciousness, and persistence with which he had met and overcome dangers, as well as his ability to execute successfully his hazardous assignment, profoundly impressed his countrymen. The written records of his expedition were published throughout the colonies and in England, resulting in widespread public praise for the young Washington.

Official negotiations had failed; a formal remonstrance had been tried in vain; now the possession of the disputed territory would be determined by the harsher methods of war. Preparations began; troops were raised in Virginia; Washington was made lieutenant colonel and entrusted with a command. Meanwhile, the French had arrived at The Fork, where they felled trees, built barracks, and laid the foundations of their new citadel, Fort Duquesne.

On May 1st, 1754, Colonel Washington set out to recapture this site by force. On May 24th, the American regiment reached the Great Meadows in southern Pennsylvania, still some sixty miles from Fort Duquesne. Here Washington was informed that a company of

BUILDING THE FORT

French soldiers was on the march to attack him and had been seen along the Youghiogheny River, only a few miles away. Washington immediately erected a small stockade to which he gave the appropriate name of Fort Necessity. After learning from the scouts of the Half-King that the approaching French company was only a scouting party, Washington determined to strike the first blow.

Two Indians had followed the trail of the French and discovered their hiding place in a rocky ravine. The Americans advanced cautiously, intending to surprise and capture the whole force, but the French were on the alert. Seeing the approaching Americans, they flew to arms. The engagement was brief but decisive against the French. The French leader Jumonville and ten of his party were killed; twenty-one were made prisoners.

WASHINGTON ATTACKING JUMONVILLE

DEATH OF JUMONVILLE (ON LEFT)

Washington returned to the Great Meadows and Fort Necessity where he waited for reinforcements. Anticipating an upcoming march against Fort Duquesne, he began to cut a road across the rough country in the direction of the French fort. A month of precious time passed during which he had extended the new road twenty miles, but only one small company of volunteers from South Carolina arrived at the camp to reinforce his undersized army. Meanwhile, the French and her allies had been collecting in great numbers at Fort Duquesne.

Although Washington's whole force numbered scarcely four hundred, he marched to dislodge the enemy from Fort Duquesne. After advancing thirteen miles, his scouts reported to him that the French general, De Villiers, was approaching with a huge army of French and Indians. Washington felt it prudent to fall back to Fort Necessity, which stood in an open meadow midway between two tree-covered knolls.

On the 3rd of July, Washington's forces had scarcely secured the fort when De Villiers and his 1,200 men arrived and surrounded the fort. The French stationed themselves on the tops of the knolls about sixty yards from the fort where they could fire down upon the Americans. Many of the Indians climbed into the treetops where they were concealed by the thick foliage. For nine hours during a rain storm, from ten in the morning until dark, a continuous shower of musket balls was poured into the fort upon the Americans.

SHOOTING DOWN THE SOLDIERS

Although thirty of Washington's men were killed, the Americans bravely resisted, returning the fire of the French with unabated vigor. At length, De Villiers proposed that the Americans surrender. Wash-

THE DOCUMENT OF SURRENDER SIGNED BY WASHINGTON AT FT. NECESSITY

ington, seeing that it would be impossible to hold out much longer, accepted the honorable terms of capitulation that were offered him by the French general. On July 4th, Washington's army, allowed to keep its equipment and provisions, marched out of the little fort they had so courageously defended and returned to Virginia.

Following his arrival from the Great Meadows, the Virginia House of Burgesses voted Colonel Washington a public thanks for the gallant stand he and his men had made in the face of overwhelming odds. The Ohio Valley was now in the undisturbed possession of the French, who continued to ravage and plunder the English trading posts and settlements along the inner frontiers.

Chapter 3

British Intervention

The British cabinet perceived that a war against the French was both eminent and inevitable, but the English colonies in America at that time still did not pose a unified threat to the French. The colonies either were too disjointed to take meaningful measures for their own common defense, or were unwilling to take upon themselves the costly task of building forts and maintaining troops.

Seeking a means to impede the French and strengthen the Americans, the British ministry instructed the colonies to cultivate the friendship of the Six Nations Indians, and to renew their treaty with the Iroquois confederacy, the most powerful of their Indian allies. The ministry also encouraged the colonial authorities to some sort of joint action against the French, recommending that they band together for their common protection and defense.

MEETING WITH THE INDIANS

Accordingly, the colonies unanimously resolved that "a union of the colonies was absolutely necessary for their preservation." Desiring that their common counsels, wealth, and strength be directed jointly against the French, a committee consisting of one representative from each colony was appointed to draw up a plan of union. On June 14th, 1754, a congress was held at Albany, New York, with delegates attending from New Hampshire, Massachusetts, Rhode Island, Connecticut, New York, Pennsylvania, and Maryland.

About one hundred and fifty Indians of the Six Nations were present at the congress; the convention made a treaty with these representatives. The convention next addressed the question of uniting the colonies in a common government. Dr. Benjamin Franklin, who attended the convention as the delegate from Pennsylvania, produced a plan subsequently titled "The Albany Plan of Union." As Dr. Franklin later recounted:

In 1754, war with France being again apprehended, a congress of commissioners from the different colonies was ... assembled at Albany, there to confer with the chiefs of the six nations concerning the means of defending both their country and ours. ... In our way thither [to Albany], I projected and drew up a plan for the union of all the colonies under one government, so far as might be necessary for defence and other important general purposes. ... It then appeared that several of the commissioners had formed plans of the same kind. ... A committee was then appointed, one member from each colony, to consider the several plans and report. Mine happened to be preferred . . . and the plan was unanimously agreed to, and copies ordered to be transmitted to the Board of Trade [in England] and to the Assemblies of several provinces.

BENJAMIN FRANKLIN

Franklin's plan bore several similarities to the later federal Constitution. Under his Albany plan, the new government would be composed both of representatives of the King and representatives from the colonial assemblies. Its president and council would be vested with the power to declare war and peace, conclude treaties with the Indian nations, regulate trade and make purchases of uninhabited lands from the Indians, settle new colonies, make laws governing those colonies until they could become separate governments, and raise troops, build forts, equip armed vessels and adopt other measures for the general defense. To accomplish these objectives, power would be given to impose any necessary duties or taxes in a means least burdensome to the people. Finally, all laws passed by the American body would be sent to England for the King's approval.

JOIN, or DIE.

FRANKLIN DREW THIS FIGURE TO
ILLUSTRATE HIS ALBANY PLAN

Franklin's plan was signed by the attending delegates on the 4th of July, 1754 (the same day Washington was retreating from Fort Necessity, and twenty-two years before another 4th of July on which Franklin voted to approve a document that he also assisted in forming — the Declaration of Independence). Copies of the Albany Plan were then distributed to each colonial assembly and sent to the King's council for approval.

FRANKLIN LATER HELPED DRAFT
AND THEN SIGNED THE DECLARATION

The response to the Albany Plan from both the British government and the colonial assemblies was the same — it was rejected. The British ministry rejected it because it gave too much power to the colonies; the colonies rejected it because it gave too much power to the King. Perhaps this rejection by both sides was the strongest proof that it steered exactly in the middle of the interests of both America and Great Britain at that time.

Having rejected the plan of union, the British ministry instead proposed to the colonial governors (most of whom were appointed directly by the King) that they, with one or more of their council, meet periodically to adopt measures for their general defense. The governors would be given power to draw on the British treasury for such sums of money as they needed, but those British funds were to be fully repaid by a tax to be imposed on the colonies. The colonies, however, were not willing to submit to this taxation by Great Britain and rejected the plan. Franklin later commented on the rejection both of his Albany Plan and of the King's substituted proposal:

> The Assemblies did not adopt it as they all thought there was too much prerogative in it; and in England it was judged to have too much of the democratic. . . . I am still of opinion it would have been happy for both sides of the water if it had been adopted. The colonies so united would have been suffi-

ciently strong to have defended themselves; there would then have been no need of troops from England; of course the subsequent pretence for taxing America and the bloody contest it occasioned would have been avoided. But such mistakes are not new; history is full of the errors of states and princes.

Even though preparations for conflict continued, there had been no official declarations of war. The ministers of France and England kept reassuring each other of peaceable intentions, but when Louis XV sent out a fleet carrying three thousand soldiers to reinforce the French army in Canada, the British government responded. King George III, pointing not

CARRYING TROOPS TO AMERICA

only to the French fleet but also to the establishment of the French forts on the Ohio and the attack upon Colonel Washington at Fort Necessity, ordered General Edward Braddock to proceed to America with two regiments of English regulars to oust the French.

Braddock, now over sixty years of age, was an Irish officer of forty years' experience. He thought well of himself and was well thought of by others, but he was not pleased with the prospect of this war. In fact, the night before he sailed from England, he went with his two aides to see a Mrs. Bellamy and left with her his will, designating her husband as his beneficiary. He unfolded a map and — displaying

GENERAL EDWARD BRADDOCK

both his anger and melancholy — complained that he was "going forth to conquer whole worlds with a handful of men, and to do so must cut his way through unknown woods." Braddock was the first British general to conduct a major campaign in a remote wilderness; he had neither historical precedents nor the experience of others to guide him.

Chapter 4

The Plans for War

On February 20th, 1755, the British troops arrived in America and dropped anchor in Hampton Roads, Virginia. The American colonists were greatly encouraged by the arrival of General Braddock and his two regiments — the first substantial force of British regulars ever to land on American soil. The colonists were now confident in the success of the campaign. It seemed to them that all that was needed to drive the French out, or to whiten American fields with French bones, was the English army.

GOVERNOR DINWIDDIE

General Braddock proceeded to Williamsburg, the capital of Virginia, to meet with Governor Dinwiddie. Braddock then issued a request that the other colonial governors travel to Virginia for a planning meeting.

Meanwhile, the strength of the two British regiments was being boosted by the enlistment of some colonials. The British 44th regiment was commanded by Sir Peter Halkett, a superb officer, while the British 48th was commanded by Colonel Dunbar, an inept and cowardly officer.

Following their initial stop at Hampton Roads, Braddock and the English fleet sailed up the Potomac to Alexandria, Virginia. There, on April 14th, Braddock met with the governors from the other colonies. The condition of colonial affairs was discussed, and it was resolved not to invade Canada but instead to repel the French on the western and northern frontiers. Plans were approved for four separate military campaigns against the French.

Lawrence, the British governor of Nova Scotia, was to secure that province according to the English version of boundaries. General Johnson in New York was to recruit and pay a force of volunteers and Mohawk Indians to capture the French post at Crown Point. Governor Shirley

FRENCH FORT AT CROWN POINT

of Massachusetts was to equip a regiment and drive the French from their fortress at Niagara, near the current location of Buffalo, New York. Finally, Braddock, the commander-in-chief of all the campaigns, would personally direct the most important effort, leading the British regulars and American volunteers against Fort Duquesne and driving the French from the Ohio Valley.

For the expedition against Nova Scotia, three thousand men under Generals Monckton and Winslow sailed from Boston on the 20th of May. On June 1st, they were reinforced by 300 more British troops and advanced against the principal French post in that region. After a bombardment of five days, the French set fire to their works and evacuated the country. With the loss of less than twenty men, the English were in possession of the whole of Nova Scotia.

The expedition led by General Johnson against Crown Point on Lake Champlain did not secure its main objective but nevertheless did provide a victory for the English soldiers in the campaign. In a major encounter near Whitehall, seven hundred of the French were killed with three hundred more wounded, while the colonies lost scarcely two hundred.

The assault against Niagara by Governor Shirley of Massachusetts and his twenty-five hundred men was started too late in the year. The troops had proceeded only as far as Osweego on Lake Ontario before the planned attack was abandoned. No further attempts were made until the following year after the formal declaration of war on June 9th, 1756.

GOVERNOR SHIRLEY

The campaign by General Braddock against Fort Duquesne was the one in which the young George Washington participated.

Washington's love for the military began early. Tradition holds that the first battles he commanded were the imaginary engagements in which he and his schoolmates played. In 1751, when Washington was nineteen, Governor Dinwiddie made him a major in the Virginia militia and gave him command of one of the four divisions into which Dinwiddie had divided the militia. Washington introduced a uniform discipline and infused his own military spirit throughout his command. He was promoted to colonel in 1754.

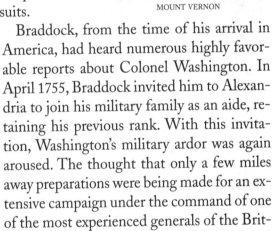

MOUNT VERNON

Shortly thereafter, however, Governor Dinwiddie reorganized the militia, allowing no rank higher than captain. Colonel Washington promptly offered his resignation and left the service in disgust. He retired to private life at Mount Vernon, now determined to spend his life there in agricultural pursuits.

YOUNG COLONEL WASHINGTON

Braddock, from the time of his arrival in America, had heard numerous highly favorable reports about Colonel Washington. In April 1755, Braddock invited him to Alexandria to join his military family as an aide, retaining his previous rank. With this invitation, Washington's military ardor was again aroused. The thought that only a few miles away preparations were being made for an extensive campaign under the command of one of the most experienced generals of the British army stirred him and made him yearn to go back to the field. Washington was eager to study military tactics under a professional soldier of such high standing.

Washington's mother, concerned for his safety, hurried to Mount Vernon to persuade him not to accept the invitation but was unable to discourage him. In their conversation, he reminded her, "The God to whom you commended me, madam, when I set out upon a more perilous errand, defended me from all harm, and I trust He will do so now. Do not you?"

After her departure, Washington left Mount Vernon for Alexandria. At Braddock's headquarters, the young colonel and the veteran general first met. Washington was welcomed into Braddock's military family with joy by Braddock's two other aides, Captains Orme and Morris.

Braddock's army was almost ready to begin its march when a difficulty arose that nearly called off the expedition. Even though American enthusiasm for Braddock's endeavor was great, the public had been reluctant to furnish the horses, teamsters, and wagons necessary for conveying military supplies and provisions during the campaign. To supply this shortage, Benjamin Franklin came to the aid of the British army.

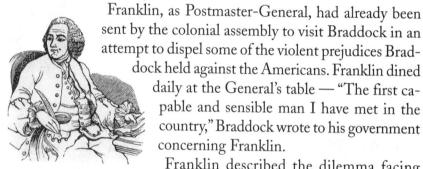

Franklin, as Postmaster-General, had already been sent by the colonial assembly to visit Braddock in an attempt to dispel some of the violent prejudices Braddock held against the Americans. Franklin dined daily at the General's table — "The first capable and sensible man I have met in the country," Braddock wrote to his government concerning Franklin.

Franklin described the dilemma facing Braddock:

BENJAMIN FRANKLIN

We found the General at Frederick, waiting impatiently for the return of those he had sent through the back parts of Maryland and Virginia to collect wagons. When I was about to depart, the returns of wagons . . . amounted only to twenty-five, and not all of those were in serviceable condition. The General and all the officers were surprised, declared the expedition was then at an end . . . and exclaimed against the [British] ministers for ignorantly landing them in a country destitute of the means of conveying their stores, baggage, etc., not less than 150 wagons being necessary. I happened to say I thought it was a pity they had not been . . . in Pennsylvania, as in that country almost every farmer had his wagon. The General eagerly laid hold of my words and said, "Then you, sir, who are a man of interest there, can probably procure them for us; and I beg you will undertake it."

Franklin then turned with great effect to Pennsylvania, a colony of prosperous small farmers who were apathetic to the war but who

ADVERTISEMENT

Lancaſter, May 6th. 1755.

NOTICE is hereby given to all who have contracted to ſendWaggons and Teams, or ſingle Horſes from *York* County to the Army at *Wills's* Creek, that *David M·Conaughy* and *Michal Schwoope* of the ſaid County, Gentlemen, will attend on my Behalf at *York* Town on *Friday* next, and at *Philip Forney's* on *Saturday*, to value or appraiſe all ſuch Waggons, Teams and Horſes, as ſhall appear at thoſe Places on the ſaid Days for that Purpoſe; and ſuch as do not then appear muſt be valued at *Wills's* Creek.

The Waggons that are valued at *York* and *Forney's*, are to ſet out immediately after the Valuation from thence for *Wills'* Creek, under the Conduct and Direction of Perſons I ſhall appoint for that Purpoſe.

The Owner or Owners of each VVaggon or Set of Horſes, ſhould bring with them to the Place of Valuation, and deliver to the Appraiſers, a Paper containing a Deſcription of their ſeveral Horſes in VVriting, with their ſeveral Marks natural and artificial; which Paper is to be annexed to the Contract.

Each VVaggon ſhould be furniſhed with a Cover, that the Goods laden therein may be kept from Damage by the Rain, and the Health of the Drivers preſerved, who are to lodge in the VVaggons. And each Cover ſhould be marked with the Contractor's Name in large Characters.

Each VVaggon, and every Horſe Driver ſhould alſo be furniſhed with a Hook or Sickle, fit to cut the long Graſs that grows in the Country beyond the Mountains.

As all the VVaggons are obliged to carry a Load of Oats, or Indian Corn, Perſons who have ſuch Grain to diſpoſe of, are deſired to be cautious how they hinder the King's Service, by demanding an extravagant Price on this Occaſion.

B. FRANKLIN.

ONE OF FRANKLIN'S MANY ADVERTISEMENTS FOR BRADDOCK

possessed abundant resources. Franklin advertised throughout local communities, explaining the generous terms of payment that the British offered the farmers for the lease of their wagons. The following excerpt is from Franklin's advertisement in Lancaster, Pennsylvania, on April 26, 1755:

> Whereas, 150 wagons, with 4 horses to each wagon, and 1,500 saddle or pack horses are wanted for the service of His Majesty's forces . . . and His Excellency, General Braddock, having been pleased to empower me to contract for the hire of the same; I hereby give notice that I shall attend . . . Lancaster from this day to next Wednesday evening, and at York from next Thursday morning till Friday evening, where I shall be ready to agree for wagons and teams, or single horses. . . . Note — My son, William Franklin, is empowered to enter into like contracts with any person in Cumberland County.

Benj. a Franklin

Franklin told them quite candidly that it would be preferable for them voluntarily to hire their wagons and teams to the British rather than waiting until they were dragooned by the British army. Franklin appealed not only to their patriotism but also to their pocketbooks — as evidenced by the following notice:

To the Inhabitants of the Counties of Lancaster, York, and Cumberland

Friends and Countrymen,

I found the General and officers extremely exasperated on account of their not being supplied with horses and carriages, which had been expected . . .

It was proposed to send an armed force immediately . . . to seize as many of the best carriages and horses as should be wanted and compel as many persons into the service as would be necessary to drive and take care of them.

I apprehended that the progress of British soldiers . . . on such an occasion (especially considering the temper they are in and their resentment against us) would be attended with many and great inconveniences to [us], and therefore [I] more willingly took the trouble of trying first what might be done by fair and equitable means . . . you [now] have an opportunity of receiving and dividing among you a very considerable sum; for if . . . this expedition should continue (as it is more than probable it will) for 120 days, the hire of these wagons and horses will amount to upwards of £30,000, which will be paid you in silver and gold of the King's money. . . .

If you are really, as I believe you are, good and loyal subjects to His Majesty, you may now do a most acceptable service and make it easy to yourselves. . . . But if you do not this service to your King and country voluntarily when such good pay and reasonable terms are offered to you, your loyalty will be strongly suspected. The King's business must be done; so many brave troops, come so far for your defence, must not

stand idle through your backwardness to do what may be rea-
sonably expected from you; wagons and horses must be had,
violent measures will probably be used. . . .

I am obliged to send word to the General in fourteen days;
and I suppose . . . a body of soldiers will immediately enter the
province for the purpose — which I shall be sorry to hear because I am very sincerely and truly your friend and well-wisher,

According to Franklin, the desired results were achieved:

In two weeks the 150 wagons with 259 carrying horses were
on their march for the camp. The advertisement promised
payment according to the valuation in case any wagon or horse
should be lost. The owners, however, alleging they did not
know General Braddock or what dependence might be had
on his promise, insisted on my [personal] bond . . . which I
accordingly gave them. The General, too, was highly satis-
fied with my conduct in procuring him the wagons . . . thank-
ing me repeatedly and requesting my further assistance in
sending provisions after him. I undertook this also and was
busily employed in it.

OBTAINING WAGONS AND SUPPLIES

Chapter 5

The Advance

With the wagons and teams now supplied, General Braddock finally set out from Alexandria, Virginia, in the latter part of April to expel the French from Fort Duquesne. With the few American troops that had joined the expedition, Braddock's army numbered nearly two thousand men, most of whom were British veterans who had seen service in the wars of Europe. Braddock briefly halted his march at Will's Creek in northwestern Maryland where he constructed Fort Cumberland, and on May 30th, he resumed his advance.

An advance party was sent forward to open a road over the rugged, forested land. Several guides led the way, followed by three hundred and fifty soldiers under Lieutenant-Colonel Thomas Gage, and then by a working party with two hundred and fifty axmen. Next came the tool-wagons, two cannons, and the rear guard, all of which comprised the advance party.

THOMAS GAGE

General Braddock trailed this detachment with the main body, the artillery, and the provisions. The wagons and artillery moved along the newly cut road, and the troops filed through the woods on both sides. The pack horses and the cattle, along with their drivers, tediously made their way amidst the trees and thickets. A body of regulars with the American provincials brought up the rear.

MARCHING THROUGH THE WOODS

The twelve-foot-wide road was opened by the advance party with strenuous effort across mountains and rocky ridges, over ravines and rivers, and through the dense forest country that stood between Braddock's force and Fort Duquesne. Because of the wagons and heavy baggage, workers were required to level the high spots and erect bridges over every creek; and the baggage and supply wagons were so heavily loaded that the horses had great difficulty pulling them over the rough cut terrain. The full army marched in a slender column behind the work crew, extending nearly four miles back along the narrow and broken road.

Because the progress was so slow, Braddock feared that the French would have time to entrench themselves in large numbers at Fort Duquesne. He considered it essential to move ahead rapidly and, if possible, surprise the French and cut them off from additional relief forces.

On June 19th, relying on the advice of Washington, Braddock left the heavy baggage behind with Colonel Dunbar and an escort of 600 men. Placing himself at the head of 1,300 select troops, Braddock proceeded by more rapid marches toward Fort Duquesne with only those things that were absolutely necessary, leaving Dunbar and his group with the wagons to follow as best they could.

Shortly after the army was split, Washington came down with a high fever that lasted for days and threatened his life. The physician was so alarmed that Braddock ordered Washington to drop out of the march until he recovered. With a wagon for his hospital, Washington remained under the physician's care. After two weeks, though not fully recovered, Washington was eager to overtake the column and decided to move forward, suffering great pain because of the constant jolting of the wagon over the rough roads.

As the army continued its march to Fort Duquesne, a band of Shawnee and Delaware Indians — faithful allies of the British — appeared. They had frequently offered to harass and attack the French and they renewed that offer, asking to help the English in the coming conflict.

Washington, knowing they would be invaluable in a battle, strongly urged General Braddock to accept their offer. The General did so, but with such a cold indifference that he offended the Indian volunteers. That initial offense was so intensified by the subsequent neglect they experienced from Braddock that the Indian volunteers soon departed. According to Franklin's account:

> This General was, I think, a brave man, and might probably have made a figure as a good officer in some European war. But he had too much self-confidence, too high an opinion of the validity of regular troops, and too [low] a one of both Americans and Indians. George Croghan, our Indian inter-

preter, joined him on his march with one hundred of those people who might have been of great use to his army as guides, scouts, etc., if he had treated them kindly; but [Braddock] slighted and neglected them, and they gradually left him.

Braddock, though not deficient in courage or in military skill, was totally unacquainted with the style of warfare necessary for the American woods. Furthermore, he was self-willed, arrogant, proud, and held the opinions of the colonial officers in contempt. Thoroughly skilled in the tactics of European warfare, he believed that battles could be fought in America as they had long been fought in Europe — that soldiers would be marched directly against their opponents on an open field of battle as if they both were on a parade ground. Franklin, however, warned General Braddock about the Indian style of warfare.

In conversation with him one day, [Braddock] was giving me some account of his intended progress. "After taking Fort Duquesne," says he, "I am to proceed to Niagara . . . for Duquesne can hardly detain me above three or four days . . . " Having before revolved in my mind the long line his army must make in their march by a very narrow road to be cut for them through the woods and bushes. . . . I had conceived some doubts and some fears. . . . But I ventured only to say, " . . . The only danger I apprehend of obstruction to your march is from the ambuscades of Indians. . . . And the slender line, near four miles long,

WAITING IN AMBUSH

which your army must make, may expose it to be attacked by surprise in its flanks, and to be cut like a thread into several pieces. . . . " He smiled at my ignorance and replied, "These savages may indeed be a formidable enemy to your raw American militia; but upon the King's regular and disciplined troops, sir, it is impossible they should make any impression." I was conscious of an impropriety in my disputing with a military man in matters of his profession and said no more.

Braddock ignored Franklin's warning. Furthermore, he could not bear to be advised by an inferior, so when Washington repeated the same warning as Franklin and pointed out the danger of ambushes and the need for scouting parties, Braddock flew into a rage. He strode up and down in his tent and said that it was high times when a colonial buckskin could teach a British general how to fight. "The Indians," said Braddock, "may frighten continental troops, but they can make no impression on the King's regulars!"

By July 7th, the column had arrived within twelve miles of Fort Duquesne and its difficulties seemed almost over. The British were confident that the French and their allies were not great in numbers, else some type of confrontation would have already occurred — especially since the Indians greatly disliked artillery and battling from within the confines of a fort.

The following day, July 8th, the forward detachment had reached the junction of the Youghiogheny and Monongahela Rivers. That evening, the friendly Indians showed themselves again to offer their services. For the second time, Washington intervened on their behalf and explained to Braddock the Indian's style of warfare, of laying ambushes and of fighting from behind trees. As scouts, they could go ahead of the army and reconnoiter the woods and ravines to uncover any waiting ambush. Washington urged Braddock to receive them, but Braddock, confident in the courage of his own troops, scorned their assistance and firmly refused their offer. He not only disdained Washington's advice, he again offended the Indians by his rudeness. His unfortunate decision sealed the fate of the following day.

Chapter 6

The Battle at the Monongahela

Early the next morning, July 9th, 1755, the British army crossed the river and continued its march along the southern shore of the Monongahela. There was no sign of any enemy. At noon, from the heights above the Monongahela, Washington looked back upon the ascending army which had just crossed the stream for the second time, now only ten miles from Fort Duquesne. The companies, in their crimson uniforms with shining weapons and floating banners, were marching gaily to cheerful music as they entered the forest.

ON THE MARCH

Washington was often heard to say that the most beautiful spectacle he ever beheld was the display of British troops on the morning of that eventful day:

> Every man was neatly dressed in full uniform; the soldiers were arranged in columns and marched in exact order; the sun gleamed from their burnished arms; the river flowed tranquilly on their right, and the deep forest overshadowed them with solemn grandeur on their left. Officers and men were equally inspirited with cheering hopes and confident anticipations.

The army, its slender line nearly four miles long, moved forward with military precision and in fine spirits. Being only a few miles from

Fort Duquesne, the troops felt certain that within a few hours they would be its master. To all appearance, the country was as uninhabited as on the morning of creation, but appearances were deceiving.

France was not willing to give up Fort Duquesne without a struggle. Even though the fort had been receiving reinforcements for two months, the French forces still were unevenly matched against Braddock's greater numbers. Even the Indian allies of the French realized the disparity between the sizes of the two armies. Having been kept abreast of Braddock's progress by the reports of their scouts, the French determined that an ambush would be their most effective defense.

The night before the battle, the French commander of Fort Duquesne, with great difficulty, persuaded the Indians to join in the ambush against the British. A force of 72 French regulars, 146 Canadian militiamen, and 637 Indians (a combined force of 855) set out from Duquesne to harass and annoy the 1,300 English, not intending to face them in serious battle. The French, already very familiar with the territory, laid an ambush at a point seven miles from the fort. They were just reaching the spot and settling into their positions when the first British troops came into sight.

READY TO LAUNCH THE AMBUSH

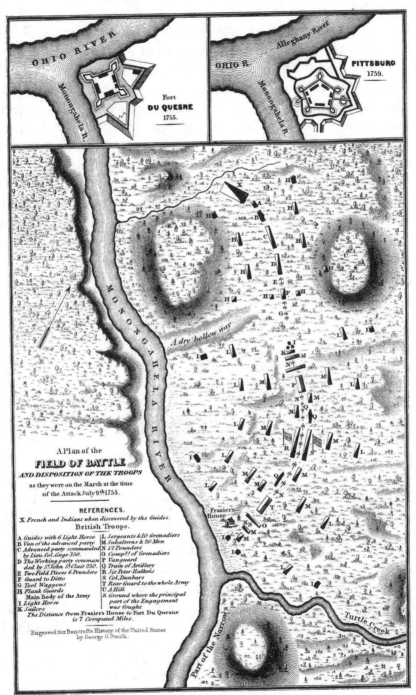

MAP OF THE BATTLE AREA

It was almost one o'clock in the afternoon; Colonel Thomas Gage's forward detachment of three hundred and fifty soldiers and two hundred and fifty workers and axmen [†] was progressing up an incline. A few guides and some small flanking parties were in the advance. General Braddock followed slightly behind this forward detachment with his columns of artillery, baggage, and the main body of the army. (Although only a small distance intervened between these first two groups of the lead division, Dunbar's division conveying the heavy baggage was now more than 40 miles to the rear.)

Gage's forward detachment had just crossed a shallow ravine with a hill and dense undergrowth on the right and a dry hollow on the left when his scouts and flanking parties came running back. At the same instant, Gordon, the engineer who was marking out the road, spotted an Indian running toward him. The Indian pulled up short and waved his hat over his head.

A quick and heavy fire was immediately heard; the enemy now revealed its presence by a discharge of weapons. A shower of musket  balls was poured into the front of Gage's company, doing extensive damage, sending metallic messengers of death among the unsuspecting soldiers. A storm of bullets, piercing flesh and shattering bones, swept the astounded ranks. To the British, it was like a supernatural attack from invisible spirits; not a musket was seen; the enemy was invisible. The blue smoke rising up after every discharge revealed that the firing came from the trees. The disconcerted British soldiers fired

AMBUSHED!

[†] Some early historical accounts indicate that Daniel Boone (1734-1820), a contemporary of George Washington, may have been a member of this work party.

back into the woods at random, but without effect, doing little more than to sliver the bark from trees and to cut saplings.

The Indians, however, were unerring marksmen, skilled in the art of ambush and guerilla warfare. Crash followed crash in rapid succession. The ground was littered with the dead and the dying. The horses, many wounded by bullets and all in a frenzy, reared and plunged and tore along the road, dragging wagons after them, trampling the living and the dead. The teamsters and axmen fled, while the soldiers remained. There was no defense that could be made; the ranks were in utter confusion. The intense, level-headed efforts of the officers to restore order were unsuccessful. A deadly storm of bullets continued to rain down upon them. The Indians were laughing derisively at the powerless struggles of their victims.

FLEEING IN CONFUSION

Gage's men panicked; the confusion became even greater. The men fired constantly, but could see no enemy. Their feeble return fire merely hit the rocks or was buried in the gigantic trees. (In the Court of Inquiry held by the British authorities after the battle, none of the English involved in the

FIRING AT AN INVISIBLE ENEMY

fight could say they had seen even a hundred of the enemy; and "many of the officers, who were in the heat of the action the whole time, would not assert that they saw one.") Yet every volley from their hidden foe flew into the crowded ranks of the British with deadly certainty.

Braddock, hearing the intensity of the firing and knowing that his forward detachment was seriously engaged, moved up rapidly with the main column, leaving Sir Peter Halkett with 400 men (including most of the Virginia provincials) to guard the baggage. Before Braddock could

TRYING TO FIRE THE CANNONS

reinforce Gage, however, Gage's men had retreated, leaving their six-pounders (cannons capable of firing six-pound projectiles) in the hands of the enemy. The retreating men collided with the advancing men and artillery coming to their aid, mixing the two regiments together and throwing the entire army into confusion.

The soldiers still were unable to see whom they were fighting. With their officers and comrades falling around them at every discharge from the woods, they became so panic-stricken that they were uncertain where to go or what to do. They therefore remained stationary, huddled together in several frightened groups in the midst of the ravine, some facing one way and some another, firing their guns at random at unseen targets. All were exposed without shelter to the bullets that pelted them like hail.

The hundred or so Virginia provincials, exhibiting greater savvy than the others, adopted the Indian style of warfare, fighting gallantly according to backwoods custom. Each man found a tree from behind which he fired whenever an arm, head, or any portion of an enemy became visible.

Braddock was furious about this skulking mode of battle — it was adverse to the rules of his profession and contrary to his ideas of courage and discipline. He issued a stern order that none of the troops should protect themselves behind trees. He then busied himself in efforts to form his men into regular platoons and columns according to the rules of military tactics, even beating his men with his sword if they attempted to take cover behind trees or fallen logs. But while he was engaged in these futile endeavors, the French and Indians, in the concealment of ravines and from behind rocks and trees, continued to single out their victims. Having a brightly colored target virtually unknown in forest warfare, they were playing deadly havoc: the beautiful red coats were targets they could not miss.

Although the typical British regular was brave in more conventional dangers, fighting a deadly enemy he could not see was something completely new. The scene was capable of intimidating the boldest of heart. The yells of the Indians, the panic of the soldiers, the frantic running of wounded horses, the unceasing rattle of musketry, the storm of leaden hail, the continual dropping of the dead, the groans of the wounded — all combined to form a scene of complete despair.

Braddock was a lion in combat. He continued undaunted while being showered with bullets, having five horses shot out from under him; yet his reckless courage was not turning the tide of the battle. His secretary was killed and both his English aides were wounded. Washington, the only uninjured aide of the general, rode over every part of the field carrying the general's orders.

Halkett's 400 men at the tail of the column were faring somewhat better than the main body, although Sir Peter Halkett himself was killed, and his son — while trying to help him — was shot dead by his side.

It was a purely Indian-style fight, more one-sided than had ever occurred in the history of woodland warfare. The pandemonium lasted over two hours. A hail of bullets that hardly tested the aim of the French and the Indians had been poured into the British army. It was butchery rather than a battle.

GEORGE WASHINGTON DELIVERING ORDERS AND DIRECTING THE TROOPS

The events occurring around Colonel Washington during the battle provide compelling evidence not only of God's care but of His direct intervention on Washington's behalf. Although Washington still had not recovered completely from his illness, he remained faithful to his duty, unflinching in the face of disaster. Carrying the general's orders to subordinates in all parts of the field made him a particularly conspicuous mark to the enemy, who did not fail to take advantage of it. One who was watching Washington during the battle reported, "I expected every moment to see him fall. Nothing but the superintending care of Providence could have saved him."

Following the battle, the Indians testified that they had specifically singled Washington out and repeatedly shot at him, but without effect. They became convinced that he was protected by an Invisible Power and that no bullet could harm him. Two horses had been shot from under him; four times his coat had been torn by musket balls; but he escaped without injury. Shielded by God's hand, he was untouched by bullet or bayonet, arrow or tomahawk, even though scores of victims fell around him.

Finally, Braddock was shot in his right side and sank to the ground wounded. He, along with the rest of the officers on horseback, had been a special target. The Indians had singled them all out and every

GENERAL BRADDOCK (CENTER) IS SHOT

mounted officer — except Washington — was slain before Braddock fell. Upon Braddock's fall, the regular troops fled in confusion. It was a race for life by every man who could drag his legs behind him. The battle became a rout. Everything was abandoned to the enemy — wagons, guns, artillery, cattle, horses, baggage, provisions, and £25,000 in specie. Even the private papers of the general were left on the field.

The forest floor behind them was strewn with the dead. The Indians emerged from their concealments with tomahawk and scalping-knife to seize their bloody trophy of scalps from the dead and from the wounded still struggling on the ground. Their tomahawks soon numbered the wounded with the slain.

Of three companies of Virginia troops, scarcely thirty men were left alive. Braddock, in his contempt, had kept the Virginians at the rear of his

A BLOODY MASSACRE

force, but Washington now organized those thirty to cover the panicked flight of the now shattered British army.

The brutality of the battle was indicated by the number of casualties. Seven hundred and fourteen of the British soldiers had been killed or wounded; of eighty-six officers, twenty-six were killed and thirty-seven more were wounded. The losses of the French and Indians were slight, amounting to only three officers and thirty men killed, and as many others wounded.

The Indians were so elated over their unexpected success and so eager to secure the rich spoils of the British that instead of pursuing the retreating army and perhaps destroying it, they remained upon the field. They had never known such a rich harvest of scalps and booty.

GATHERING SCALPS

BRADDOCK CARRIED FROM THE FIELD OF BATTLE

Braddock, unable to mount a horse, was hurried from the field in a litter. About a mile from the scene, his wounds were dressed. Washington now took charge, and the remnants of the army continued to retreat, planning to rejoin with the heavy baggage division under Dunbar, now the senior British military official, forty miles to the rear.

For days Braddock lingered in great pain. According to Franklin:

> Captain Orme, who was one of the General's aides-de-camp, and being grievously wounded, was brought off with [Braddock] and continued with him to his death, which happened in a few days, told me that [Braddock] was totally silent all the first day and at night only said, "Who would have thought it?"; that he was silent again the following day, only saying at last, "We shall better know how to deal with them another time," and died a few minutes after.

Braddock, who was being treated by Dr. James Craik, a close personal friend of Washington, died near the Great Meadows, a mile west of Fort Necessity. During the night, Washington read the fu-

WASHINGTON READING SCRIPTURES OVER THE HURRIED BURIAL OF BRADDOCK

neral service of the church over his grave by torchlight. Braddock was buried in the middle of the road and wagons were rolled over the fresh mound of dirt to keep his remains from being found and desecrated by any Indians that might pursue.

No attempt, however, was ever made at pursuit by the Indians. With the army of Braddock annihilated, the French, conscious that the British army posed no imminent threat, left the starving, staggering, bleeding remains to struggle back to Virginia. The victors returned to Fort Duquesne (the Indian chiefs wearing the coats, boots, and decorations of the slain British officers) to rejoice over their unexpected victory and to prepare for another assault — should the British attempt to return.

Colonel James Smith, an English officer captured before the battle, was being held captive at Fort Duquesne throughout this affair. His personal narrative provides a vivid portrayal of the scenes that transpired at the fort before, during, and after the battle. He reported that Indian scouts for the French were constantly watching the British army from mountain crags and from within the depths of the forest. Every day, runners returned to the fort with their report.

Late in the afternoon of July 9th (the day of the battle), the triumphant shouts of fleet-footed runners were heard in the forest, bringing the initial news of the great victory. They reported that the English were huddled together in a narrow ravine from which escape was almost impossible and that they were in utter confusion. The concealed Indians were shooting down the British as fast as they could load and fire; before sundown all would be killed.

Later, a larger band of about a hundred Indians appeared at the fort, yelling and shrieking in boisterous joy. It was the greatest victory they had ever known or imagined. The Indians were stunned, even shocked, at both the quantity and the richness of their plunder. Braddock's army had been laden not only with all the conveniences but with many luxuries as well — it was more than the Indians could carry away. They returned to the fort stooping beneath the load of caps, canteens, muskets, swords, bayonets, and rich uniforms that they had stripped from the dead. Most had dripping, bloody scalps, and several had money. Colonel Smith wrote:

SPORTING THE SPOILS OF VICTORY

Those that were coming in and those that had arrived kept a constant firing of small arms, and also of the great guns in the fort, which was accompanied by the most hideous shouts and yells from all quarters; so that it appeared to me as if the infernal regions had broken loose. About sundown I beheld a small party coming in with about a dozen prisoners, stripped naked, with their hands tied behind their backs. Their faces, and parts of their bodies were blackened. These prisoners they burned to death on the banks of the Allegheny river, opposite to the

BURNING THE PRISONERS

fort. I stood on the fort walls until I beheld them begin to burn one of these men. They tied him to a stake and kept touching him with fire-brands, red-hot irons, etc., and he screaming in the most doleful manner. The Indians, in the meantime, were yelling like infernal spirits. As this scene was too shocking for me to behold, I returned to my lodgings, both sorry and sore. The morning after the battle, I saw Braddock's artillery brought into the fort. The same day also I saw several Indians in the dress of British officers, with the sashes, half moons, laced hats, etc., which the British wore.

Chapter 7

Return to Fort Cumberland

The terrorized retreating British regulars finally arrived at Dunbar's camp far to the rear. The panic they brought with them instantly gripped Dunbar and his troops and the scene became one of total confusion.

Since two of the three British military leaders were now dead (Braddock and Halkett), the command of all the remaining forces fell upon the last British leader, Dunbar — a man of incompetence and no courage. Although he still had almost 1,000 men, he made no attempt to recover any of the lost provisions.

On July 12th, pretending to have the orders of the dying general, Dunbar ordered the remainder of the artillery, ammunition, heavy baggage, and provisions to be destroyed so that he would have additional horses to assist his hurried retreat to Fort Cumberland in northwestern Maryland, one hundred and twenty miles away.

SAFETY AT THE FORT

On July 17th, Washington and the disconsolate army reached Fort Cumberland. Several fugitives had already arrived and spread reports of the disaster throughout the countryside. Washington, knowing the terrible anxiety of his family, immediately wrote his mother.

July 18, 1755

Honored Madam:

As I doubt not but you have heard of our defeat, and perhaps had it represented in a worse light, if possible, than it deserves, I have taken this earliest opportunity to give you some account of the engagement as it happened, within ten miles of the French fort, on Wednesday the 9th . . .

We marched to that place without any considerable loss, having only now and then a straggler picked up by the French and scouting Indians. When we came there, we were attacked by a party of French and Indians . . . our [force] consisted of about one thousand three hundred well-armed troops, chiefly regular soldiers, who were struck with such a panic that they behaved with more cowardice than it is possible to conceive. The officers behaved gallantly in order to encourage their men, for which they suffered greatly, there being nearly sixty killed and wounded; a large proportion of the number we had.

The Virginia troops showed a good deal of bravery and were nearly all killed; for I believe out of three companies that were there, scarcely thirty men are left alive. Captain Peyrouny and all his officers down to a corporal were killed.

Captain Polson had nearly as hard a fate, for only one of his was left. In short, the dastardly behavior of those they call regulars exposed all others that were inclined to do their duty to almost certain death; and, at last, in spite of all the efforts of the officers to the contrary, they ran as sheep pursued by dogs and it was impossible to rally them.

The General was wounded, of which he died three days after. Sir Peter Halkett was killed in the field, where died many other brave officers. I luckily escaped without a wound, though I had four bullets through my coat and two horses shot under me. Captains Orme and Morris, two of the aids-de-camp, were wounded early in the engagement, which rendered the duty harder upon me as I was the only person then left to dis-

WASHINGTON'S MOTHER
OFTEN PRAYED FOR HIM

tribute the General's orders, which I was scarcely able to do as I was not half recovered from a violent illness that had confined me to my bed and a wagon for above ten days. I am still in a weak and feeble condition, which induces me to halt here two or three days in the hope of recovering a little strength to enable me to proceed homewards; from whence, I fear, I shall not be able to stir till toward September. . . .

I am, honored Madam, your most dutiful son.

G. Washington

On the same day, he wrote his brother, John A. Washington:

As I have heard since my arrival at this place [Fort Cumberland] a circumstantial account of my death and dying speech, I take this early opportunity of contradicting the first and of assuring you that I have not as yet composed the latter. But by the all-powerful dispensations of Providence I have been protected beyond all human probability or expectation; for I had four bullets through my coat and two horses shot under me yet escaped unhurt, although death was leveling my companions on every side of me!

To Governor Dinwiddie, he wrote of what he called the "dastardly behavior" of the regulars, saying:

They broke and ran as sheep before hounds, leaving the artillery, ammunition, provisions, baggage, and in short everything a prey to the enemy; and when we endeavored to rally them . . . it was with as little success as if we had attempted to stop the wild bears of the mountains, or the rivulets with our feet.

On his arrival at Fort Cumberland, Dunbar received requests from the Governors of Virginia, Maryland, and Pennsylvania to post British troops along the frontiers to offer some protection to the settlers. Dunbar, however, felt he should enter winter quarters with his troops

— even though it was still summer and winter was months away! Dunbar therefore evacuated Fort Cumberland and withdrew the regulars to Philadelphia to encamp for the winter, leaving the whole frontier open to the pillage of the French and Indians. Regarding Dunbar's decision, Benjamin Franklin quipped:

> Dunbar continued his hasty march through all the country, not thinking himself safe till he arrived at Philadelphia where the inhabitants could protect him. This whole transaction gave us Americans the first suspicion that our exalted ideas of the prowess of British regulars had not been well founded.

Franklin had issued large personal bonds for the wagons he had secured for General Braddock. With the destruction of these wagons and horses, the owners understandably pressed Franklin to make restitution for their loss, unwilling to wait for British reimbursement. Franklin, having already advanced considerable money for the campaign, was unable to pay all the notes at once. The owners therefore began to sue Franklin, which could have led to his ruin. Franklin described the tenuous situation and its resolution:

FRANKLIN

> As soon as the loss of the wagons and horses was generally known, all the owners came upon me for the valuation which I had given bond to pay. Their demands gave me a great deal of trouble. I acquainted them that the money was ready in the [British] paymaster's hands, but that orders for paying it must first be obtained from General Shirley, and that I had applied for it . . . and they must have patience. All this was not sufficient to satisfy, and some began to sue me. General Shirley at length relieved me from this terrible situation by appointing commissioners to examine the claims and ordering payment. They amounted to near £20,000, which to pay would have ruined me.

Chapter 8

The Celebrated Epilogue

If the advice Washington offered Braddock had been followed, and if the Indians had been used as scouts before the advancing army, the ambush undoubtedly would have been discovered; and it is quite possible that a victory might have been secured by the British instead of the French. But due in large part to the foolish and haughty arrogance of Braddock, the British were crushed in a bloody and infamous defeat. This, however, resulted in no disgrace to Washing-

BRADDOCK

ton. His fearlessness, perception, and quick decisions in the heat of the battle were praised in the strongest terms by his fellow officers and soldiers. Because of Divine intervention, Washington gathered acclaim and honor from the same field where his commander received only dishonor and death.

As time passed after the great battle, several facts surfaced that not only gave a better perspective to the drama that had surrounded Washington during the battle but also provided further evidence of the extent to which God had directly intervened in Washington's behalf. For example, one famous Indian warrior who was a leader in the attack was often heard to testify, "Washington was never born to be killed by a bullet! I had seventeen fair fires at him with my rifle, and after all could not bring him to the ground!" When one considers that a rifle aimed by an experienced marksman rarely misses its target, his utterance seems to have been prophetic. It was evident that an Invisible Hand turned aside the bullets.

A separate and additional verification was provided through the testimony of Mary Draper Ingels. She was kidnapped from her home in Draper Meadows, Virginia, on July 8th, 1755, by a band of Shawnee Indians. Her biography details the amazing account of her capture and subsequent midwinter escape from the Shawnees after being held captive for several months. Her return trek to civilization covered a grueling 1,000 miles.

She recounts that one day during her captivity at the Indian camp, the French held a council with the Indians. After the council concluded, the Frenchmen were talking excitedly to each other, gesturing animatedly. Mary listened to their conversation, which focused on George Washington. Having personally met Washington, she began to inquire of the Frenchmen about him. They related the account of an Indian chief named Red Hawk who had been in the victory at Duquesne. Red Hawk told of shooting eleven different times at Washington without killing him. At that point, because his gun had never before missed its mark before, he ceased firing at him, being convinced that the Great Spirit protected Washington. The Frenchmen continued to tell her more details about the battle and its final grizzly outcome. She doubted their account — surely the British could not have been so completely crushed.

TELLING THE
AMAZING STORY

After her return to civilization, she related what she had heard about the incident with Washington. Those in the settlement assured her that what the Frenchmen had told her was indeed accurate.

So remarkable was Washington's escape from the numerous perils to which he was exposed during the battle that special mention of this circumstance was made in a sermon preached shortly after the battle by the Rev. Samuel Davies, who later became the president of Princeton University. After commending the military qualities that the Virginia provincials had displayed during the fight, Davies added, "I may point out to the public that heroic youth, Colonel Washington, whom

REV. SAMUEL DAVIES

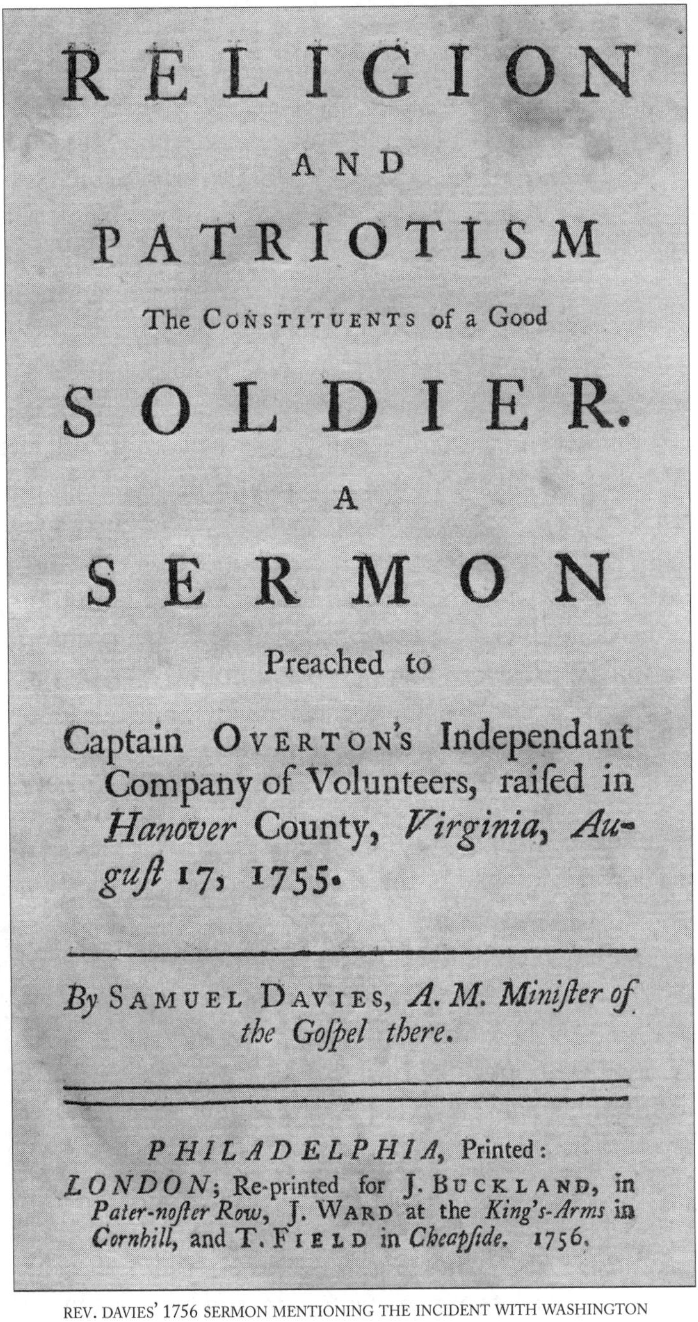

R E L I G I O N

A N D

P A T R I O T I S M

The Constituents of a Good

S O L D I E R.

A

S E R M O N

Preached to

Captain Overton's Independant Company of Volunteers, raised in *Hanover* County, *Virginia, August* 17, 1755.

By Samuel Davies, *A. M. Minifter of the Gofpel there.*

PHILADELPHIA, Printed:
LONDON; Re-printed for J. Buckland, in *Pater-nofter Row,* J. Ward at the *King's-Arms* in *Cornhill,* and T. Field in *Cheapfide.* 1756.

REV. DAVIES' 1756 SERMON MENTIONING THE INCIDENT WITH WASHINGTON

this End that you fhould be at Peace with God, and your own Confcience, and prepared for your future State. Guilt is naturally timerous, and often ftruck into a

* As a remarkable Inftance of this, I may point out to the Public that heroic Youth Col. *Wafhington*, whom I cannot but hope Providence has hitherto preferved in fo fignal a Manner, for fome important Service to his Country.

WASHINGTON'S PROTECTION BY GOD CITED IN THE SERMON

I cannot but hope Providence has hitherto preserved in so signal a manner for some important service to his country." How accurately this wish was fulfilled is evidenced by Washington's subsequent life.

And then fifteen years after the battle, Washington and Dr. Craik, a close friend of Washington from his boyhood to his death, were traveling toward the western territories to explore uninhabited regions. While near the junction of the Great Kanawha and Ohio Rivers on the border of what is now Ohio and West Virginia, a company of Indians, led by an old, respected chief, approached them. A council fire was kindled and the chief addressed Washington through an interpreter. The chief first explained that after being informed of Washington's approach to that part of the country, he set out on his long journey to meet Washington personally and to speak to him about the battle fifteen years earlier. Through the interpreter he said:

I am a chief and ruler over my tribes. My influence extends to the waters of the great lakes and to the far blue mountains. I have traveled a long and weary path that I might see the young warrior of the great battle. It was on the day when the white man's blood mixed with the streams of our forest that I first beheld this chief [Washington]. I called to my young men and said, mark yon tall and daring warrior? He is not of the red-coat tribe — he hath an Indian's wisdom, and his warriors fight as we do — himself is alone exposed. Quick, let your aim be certain, and he dies. Our rifles were leveled, rifles which, but for you, knew not how to miss

— 'twas all in vain; a power mightier far than we shielded you. Seeing you were under the special guardianship of the Great Spirit, we immediately ceased to fire at you. I am old and soon shall be gathered to the great council fire of my fathers in the land of shades; but ere I go, there is something bids me speak in the voice of prophecy. Listen! The Great

PROTECTED IN BATTLE

Spirit protects that man [pointing at Washington], and guides his destinies — he will become the chief of nations, and a people yet unborn will hail him as the founder of a mighty empire. I am come to pay homage to the man who is the particular favorite of Heaven and who can never die in battle.

Eighty years after the battle, a gold seal of Washington, containing his initials, was found on the battlefield. It had been shot off him by a bullet. (That relic is now in the possession of his family.) True to the Indian's voice of prophecy, and because God sovereignly and Divinely protected him, Washington not only did not die in that battle, he was not even wounded in any of the numerous battles in which he fought. [†] As the old Indian had prophesied, Washington did indeed become the chief of a nation, hailed by subsequent generations as a founder — in fact, as *the* Father — of his country. ■

[†] In 1779 during the American Revolution at the Battle of Brandywine, British Major Patrick Ferguson, head of the British sharpshooters, held an American officer dead in his sights at close range but instead of firing, he obeyed a strong impulse not to shoot. Ferguson did not realize at that time whom he had in his sights, but he later discovered from the soldiers with him that it was George Washington he had allowed to live. Ferguson subsequently explained: "I could have lodged half a dozen balls in him before he was out of my reach . . . but it was not pleasant to fire at the back of an unoffending individual who was acquitting himself very coolly of his duty — so I let him live." As historian Lyman Draper observed in 1881: "Had Washington fallen, it is difficult to calculate its probable effect upon the result of the struggle of the American people. How slight, oftentimes, are the incidents which, in the course of human events, seem to give direction to the most momentous concerns of the human race. This singular impulse of Ferguson illustrates, in a forcible manner, the over-ruling hand of Providence in directing the operation of a man's mind when he himself is least aware of it."

Time Line of Events

1749-1753	Numerous boundary disputes occur between British and French traders
1753	Britain directs her American colonies to seek friendship with the Six Nations Indians and to form a union among the colonies
31 Oct. 1753	George Washington departs for the French Commander General St. Pierre with a letter from Governor Dinwiddie
12 Dec. 1753	Washington arrives at the French camp
16 Jan. 1754	Washington returns to Williamsburg
Spring 1754	France reinforces troops in Canada
2 April 1754	Washington leads troops from Alexandria to Will's Creek in first step of repulsing the French
1 May 1754	Washington marches to the Great Meadows
24 May 1754	Washington reaches Great Meadows and constructs Fort Necessity
27 May 1754	Washington captures a French detachment near Fort Necessity
14 June 1754	Council convenes at Albany to construct a plan of union between the colonies
3 July 1754	Battle at Fort Necessity; Washington attacked by French forces under De Villiers
4 July 1754	Albany plan is approved by commissioners and sent to both the colonies and Great Britain for approval
	Washington surrenders and withdraws from Fort Necessity
20 Feb. 1755	General Edward Braddock arrives in Hampton Roads, Virginia

14 April 1755	Braddock meets with colonial governors in Alexandria, Virginia; four-pronged campaign against the French is planned
April 1755	General Braddock meets George Washington
20 April 1755	Braddock leaves Alexandria for Will's Creek
10 May 1755	Braddock constructs Fort Cumberland at Will's Creek
30 May 1755	Braddock leaves Fort Cumberland for Fort Duquesne
19 June 1755	Braddock, at Washington's suggestion, divides the army and begins to press forward, leaving Dunbar and the heavy baggage to follow
9 July 1755	The Battle at the Monongahela; British slaughtered
12-15 July 1755	General Braddock dies
	Dunbar destroys remaining artillery and baggage
17 July 1755	Washington and troops return to Fort Cumberland
18 July 1755	Washington writes members of his family to inform them personally of the battle
Aug. 1755	Dunbar enters winter quarters with the British troops
1770	George Washington and Dr. Craik return to the same vicinity as the battle and are met by an Indian chief

Bibliography

Abbot, John S. C. *George Washington*. New York: Dodd, Mead and Company, 1875, 1903, 1917, pp. 78-107.

Bancroft, George. *History of the United States* (10 Volumes). Boston: Little, Brown and Company, 1858, Vol. IV, pp. 182-206.

Banvard, Joseph. *Tragic Scenes in the History of Maryland and the Old French War.* Boston: Gould and Lincoln, 1856, pp. 142-173.

Bailey, Rev. J. D. *Commanders at Kings Mountain.* Gaffney, S. C.: Ed. H. Decamp, 1926, pp. 380-382.

Barker, Eugene C.; Webb, Walter P.; and Dodd, William. *The Growth of A Nation.* Evanston, Ill.: Row, Peterson, and Company, 1934, pp. 126-130.

Bellamy, Francis Rufus. *The Private Life of George Washington.* New York: Thomas Y. Crowell Co., 1951, pp. 63-116.

Bradley, A. G. *The Fight with France for North America,* "The Defeat of Braddock (1755)," Westminster: Archibald, Constable & Co., 1902, pp. 75-106.

Brooks, Elbridge S. *The True Story of George Washington.* Boston: Lothrop, Lee and Shepard Co., 1895, p. 43-64.

Custis, George Washington Parke. *Recollections and Private Memoirs of Washington,* Benson J. Lossing, editor, New York: Derby & Jackson, 1860, pp. 158-162, pp. 374-376.

Draper, Lyman C. *King's Mountain and Its Heroes.* Cincinnati: Peter Thomson, 1983, reprint 1881 original, pp. 52-54.

Franklin, Benjamin. *Works of the Late Doctor Benjamin Franklin Consisting of His Life, Written by Himself, Together with Essays, Humorous, Moral & Literary.* Dublin: P. Wogan, P. Byrne, J. Moore, and W. Jones, 1793, pp. 122-127.

Goodrich, Samuel G. *Goodrich's Pictorial History of the United States.* Philadelphia: E. H. Butler & Co., ante 1856, pp. 120-132.

Halsey, Francis W., editor. *Great Epochs in American History* (10 Volumes). New York and London: Funk and Wagnalls Company, 1912, Vol. III: *The French War and The Revolution: 1745-1782,* pp. 3-65, especially pp. 39-50.

Harland, Marion. *The Story of Mary Washington.* Boston: Houghton, Mifflin, and Company, 1893, p. 91-98.

Harrison, James A. *George Washington: Patriot, Soldier, Statesman.* New York: G. P. Putnam's Sons, 1906, pp. 53-106, especially pp. 65-102.

Headley, J. T. *The Illustrated Life of Washington.* New York: G & F Bill, 1861, pp. 25-99, especially pp. 55-64.

Irving, Washington. *The Life of George Washington* (4 Volumes). New York: Thomas Y. Crowell & Co., 1855, Vol. 1, pp. 43-191, especially pp. 163-184.

Johnson, William J. *George Washington the Christian*. Milford, Mich.: Mott Media, 1976 reprint, 1919 original, pp. 39-42.

Johonot, James. *The Stories of Our Country*. New York: American Book Company, 1887, pp. 85-94.

Ketchum, Richard M. *The World of George Washington*. New York: American Heritage Publishing Co., 1974, pp. 30-57.

Lemisch, L. Jesse, editor. *Benjamin Franklin; The Autobiography and Other Writings*. New York: New American Library, 1961, pp. 140-155.

Lossing, Benson J. *The Pictorial Field Book of the Revolution* (2 Volumes). New York: Harper & Brothers, Publishers, 1852, Vol. II, pp. 472-481.

Lossing, Benson J. *Mount Vernon and Its Associations*. New York: W. A. Townsend & Company, 1859, pp. 41-44.

Marshall, John. *Life of George Washington* (2 Volumes). Philadelphia: Crissy & Markley, and Thomas, Cowperthwait and Co., 1850, Vol. I, pp. 7-12.

Ridpath, John Clark. *Popular History of the United States of America*. Cincinnati, Philadelphia, Chicago, Memphis, Atlanta: Jones Brothers & Co., 1876, pp. 247-261.

Riviore, Mario. *The Life and Times of Washington*. Philadelphia: Curtis Publishing Co., 1967, pp. 11-15.

Schull, W. E., editor. *The Story of Our Country: Its Progress and Achievements*. Philadelphia: World Bible House, 1896, p. 136-139.

Steele, Joel Dorman; Steele, Esther Baker. *A Brief History of the United States*. New York: American Book Company, 1871, 1879, 1880, and 1885 by A. S. Barnes and Co. 1889, and American Book Company, 1900, p. 84-85.

Sparks, Jared. *The Life of George Washington*. Boston: Ferdinand Andrews, 1839, pp. 18-66.

Thom, James Alexander. *Follow the River*. New York: Ballentine Books, 1981, pp. 120-121, 369.

Thwaites, Reuben Gold, and Kendall, Calvin Noyes. *A History of the United States for Grammar Schools*. Boston: Houghton Mifflin Co., 1912, p. 127.

Washington, George. *The Writings of George Washington*, Sparks, Jared, editor (12 Vols., 1834-1837), Vol. II, pp. 88-89, pp. 468-476.

Weaver, G. S. *The Lives and Graves of Our Presidents*. Chicago: The National Book Concern, 1897, pp. 48-54.

Weems, M. L. *The Life of George Washington*. Philadelphia: H. C. Carey & I. Lea, 1824, pp. 34-43.

Willard, Emma. *Abridged History of the United States*. New York: A. S. Barnes and Burr, 1859, pp. 158-161.

Willard, Emma. *History of the United States*. Philadelphia: A. S. Barnes, and Co., 1844, pp. 121-131.

WallBuilders' Sampler
A few of our resources . . .

To learn about <u>ALL</u> our great resources,
visit **www.wallbuilders.com**
or call **800-873-2845** for a free catalog.

<u>Books</u> such as . . .

 *Original Intent: The Courts, the Constitution, & Religion* (B16) $12.95

 Celebrate Liberty! Famous Patriotic Speeches & Sermons (B30) $10.95

<u>Reprints</u> such as . . .

 Lives of the Signers of the Declaration of Independence (B14) $10.95

 Noah Webster's "Advice to the Young" (B10) $6.95

<u>DVDs</u> such as . . .

 *America's Godly Heritage* (60 min.) Also available on video, audio, and as a book (DVD01) $19.95

 *Foundations of American Government* (25 min.) Also available on video, audio, and as a book (DVD04) $9.95

<u>Videos</u> such as . . .

 *A Spiritual Heritage Tour of the US Capitol* (approx. 120 min.) Also available on DVD, audio, and as a book (V02) $19.95

 Setting the Record Straight (over 2 hrs.) Also available on DVD and as a book (V06) $19.95